EVERY HORSE HAS A STORY

AMBER SAWYER

Every Horse Has A Story

Written by Amber Sawyer
Illustrated by Tami Joe DeLisle
Contributing Editor: Amber Sawyer
Editor: Griffin Mill
Author Photo: Edward Cockroft
Digital Imaging of Illustrations by Keith Glasgow
www.glasgowphoto.com
Cover illustration based on original photo of Kendalynn Brummond, by her mother, Kelly Brummond.

ISBN: 978-1-957351-70-4

PUBLISHED BY NICO 11 PUBLISHING & DESIGN

MUKWONAGO, WISCONSIN

www.nico11publishing.com

Quantity order requests can be emailed to:

mike@nico11publishing.com

Printed in The United States of America

To the thousands of new friends I've made nationwide, to all the wonderful teachers, students, librarians, racetrack family I've met with my first book and to all that encouraged me to write another, this is for you.

TABLE OF CONTENTS

Introduction…1

1. A Racehorse Prayer…7

2. What it Feels Like to be on a Horse…9

3. In the Right Hands…11

4. Superstitious Minds…15

5. Louie, Louie…17

6. So Much in Common…21

7. Respect…23

8. Grandpa's Promise…27

9. Second Chances, Lakota's Story…29

10. Hope…33

11. Just a Brown Horse…35

12. Hot Shot…37

13. Written in the Stars…39

14. Small and Mighty Sophie…43

15. A Horse's Life on Race Day…45

16. Double Duty…49

17. Angels Everywhere…51

18. The Letter…55

19. A Ghost Story…59

20. The Artist…63

21. Life Lessons…65

22. Age is Just a Number…67

23. A Day in My Life…71

24. Horses in Heaven…75

25. The Chestnut…77

26. The Trio…82

27. The Ultimate Prize…85

28. Winning Our Race…87

29. Molly…91

30. The Tale of Derek…95

EVERY HORSE HAS A STORY

INTRODUCTION

There's a saying that goes, "Only a racehorse can take thousands of people for a ride at the same time." (Author unknown.) This is so true, and as you read this book—whether it be a story about a draft horse, a trail horse, a rodeo horse, or a racehorse—you, too, are taken along on the ride of all of these magnificent creatures in this book. Their lives have now become a part of yours, and some will give you feelings you will never forget.

Hi y'all! Thank you so much for reading my book. I hope you enjoyed it as much as I enjoyed writing it. My passion for horses began at an early age. Every little girl dreams of having a horse, and I have lived that dream almost my entire life. My passion for horses lies in the sport of harness racing and the Standardbred breed. Quite a few stories in this book reflect that passion, as I grew up in a harness racing family. As a little girl, I would ride on my dad's lap on the jog cart as he brought his horses back from the track to the barn. After I graduated high school, I raced horses all over the Midwest and up and down the East Coast and many of the connections I met in my travels inspired a good number of the stories in this book.

My first book, *Love to Race*, was one of the stories that changed my life forever. Had had it not been for my love of harness racing, I never would have met Derek Bromac N, the subject of my first book and one of the most special horses to have graced my life. *Love to Race* was written to help me get through a difficult time. (We all remember 2020 right?) There was so much more going on for me than just the pandemic, and focusing on my book was a positive light. What started off as a small, personal project, with hopes no higher than having my friends and family read it, grew to more than I could

ever have imagined. Derek and I started a program called, "Reading With a Racehorse," and to date we have traveled thousands of miles across my home state of Wisconsin. I made stops at over 100 schools and libraries, meeting thousands of children, and even inspiring a few authors! Derek traveled with me across the state, but my little book, *Love to Race*, took me so much further than that. I've spoken in nearly 300 schools and libraries to date, traveled

nearly half the country, and visited almost 25 different race tracks. I've been featured in newspapers, magazines, radio interviews, and too many TV and YouTube segments to count. I've had the privilege to tour so much of this beautiful country, from the Dakotas, to Virginia, to the beautiful, breathtaking coast of Maine, and every state in between!

On my book tours, I visit some of the most amazing sites and gorgeous landscapes, and I stay a few extra minutes to reflect on the reality that none of this would have been possible if it hadn't been for my little children's book and that old racehorse. The people I've met, the friends I've made, and the children I have inspired are memories that will last a lifetime and made me so thankful to be able to do what I do. Who would have imagined my first book would take me this far?

There are a few instances that stand out from my travels.

I met a woman in Nebraska who wrote a story, but was too apprehensive to have it published. We spoke about my experiences as an author and I'm proud to say that she is now published and performing book readings of her children's book in the Cornhusker State. I'm so happy for her! Two of the stories in this book were gifts from children I've met in my journeys. I met a high school student at a library in Pennsylvania who couldn't wait to meet me. She admitted to researching the writing process online, but nothing compared to the opportunity to meet a real, published author in person to have her questions answered. I gave her my phone number and told her to send me her book when it's published. I can't wait to read it; her story was so touching. I know she'll do great things.

I could write a novel just on all the wonderful people that have touched my life, and maybe someday I will. The idea for this book came about earlier this year, while traveling to a few book signings in Ohio, with plenty of windshield-time in front of me, it dawned on me, why not write another book? And here it is, a year later, *Every Horse Has a Story* is in your hands; a collection of stories from across the country. These are all true stories, told from the heart of their owners, and some are my own personal experiences. The past year for me has had its challenges, but when I wasn't busy working, touring, or scheduling, every minute of spare time this past year has been dedicated to what you are holding in your hands. I can't wait to see where *Every Horse Has a Story* will take me!

My favorite part of writing is all the new connections I make and the friendships that have come about, all thanks to our mutual love of horses. Horse people truly are one big family, some of them you just haven't met yet.

What happens next? You'll have to wait and see!

A RACEHORSE PRAYER

As I head to the gate for the very last time,

and the driver behind me picks up the lines,

I can hear the starter call my name out loud,

and I turn to post parade, ever so proud.

The announcer tells the crowd my name.

My life without racing just won't be the same.

I look back on my life, all the races I've done,

some that I've lost and others I've won.

I'll miss the racetrack and the call to the post,

but it's the cheer of the fans that I'll miss the most.

I'll find a new job when my racing days are through,

I am, after all, a Standardbred; there's nothing I can't do.

So please keep in mind as you take off my tack,

give me one last look at my beloved racetrack.

Written by Amber Sawyer.

WHAT IT FEELS LIKE TO BE ON A HORSE

Horses. Beautiful living creatures. Beautiful flowing manes and tails. If anybody rides horses they know what it feels like. It feels like you are flying. High, fast in the breeze. It feels like you're one with the horse. Gliding across the ground, fast in the wind. There is really no way to explain it. No way. All that I can say is that it feels amazing. It feels like you have power behind you and underneath you. It doesn't matter if your horse is tall or short, all that matters is you are confident. You have to be confident to get up on that horse and ride. You really have to trust your horse to take care of you. If you're scared, just remember to be fearless.

Written by Brynn B., age 10,
Lomira Elementary School,
Lomira, Wisconsin.

This beautiful short poem was a gift during an author visit at a small elementary school. She was so excited to present it to me.
-Amber

IN THE RIGHT HANDS

The bay, 3-year-old Standardbred colt came tearing off the racetrack uncontrollably, at a speed so fast his driver had to point him towards a wall to stop him. It took the driver behind him holding the sulky, a groom at his head, and one horseman on each side to unhook him from his sulky. With a chain over his nose and the whites of his eyes boldly showing, he was led to the bath stall to be unharnessed and bathed after the 3 year old Iowa Bred Pacing Finals at Prairie Meadows Harness Track in Altoona, Iowa, on that cool, fall September evening. His owner, Bobby Williams, a poor horsemen originally from Mississippi, spoke calmly to him, never raising his voice or showing any fear of the high-strung young pacer. He knew this was the last time he would ever take his harness off and wanted their last moments together to be the best they could possibly be. They had only been together for a few short summer months, and his horse, Khaki's Fancy, had earned enough points on the summer racing circuit to qualify for the finals. However, with winter fast approaching, Bobby knew the expense of feeding a horse over the winter was more than he could afford. He decided to send the horse to me to live in Wisconsin and race on the Wisconsin County Fair circuit. We had met earlier in the season and become fast friends. The price? Absolutely free!

"Take care of my boy, he's had a rough start in life." His eyes glistened as he gave his friend a final pat on the neck and a kiss on his nose. I had no idea the journey I was about to embark on as we loaded him in the trailer. The horse, who had been nicknamed Mikey, had a challenging start to his racing career. His previous trainer, (not Bobby) was in a rush to qualify him for his high money 2 year old Iowa Stake races. His high strung, young nature often resulted in him breaking stride behind the starting gate at the start of the race.

He would lose ground, putting him out of contention. Harness racing horses are not allowed to go off-stride in a race, they must remain on gate, either a trot or pace. It was the last race of the year and we had all winter to get to know each other before the county fair races started the following summer.

The next summer came, and Mikey was ready for the races, but I still didn't have the courage to drive him in a race. With the leading driver behind him in the sulky, I had high hopes that the winter off had broken him of his old habits. That hope was shattered quickly. Mikey went to the starting gate, the other horses lined up on either side of him, the starter said, "Go!" and off stride he went! The next week we tried again with a new, equally experienced driver. The same thing happened. And again, the following week.

Now I was frustrated and upset, a little angry, and most of all, determined. I thought to myself, *I'm going to show these boys up, and just drive him myself.* I was one of the only regular women drivers in Wisconsin. I made some calls, asked some questions, and did some research. I found out that my boy had been in an accident and went down on the track in an accident behind the starting gate as a 2 year old. When the other horses lined up next to him, he got nervous being crowded and went off stride. It was the only time in the race he did it. It was time to try a new strategy. He needed to start over. Mikey needed to learn how to be in a race and do it the right way.

"Let's just get through this race," I whispered in his ear. "I don't care where you finish, just keep me safe on the track." That's exactly what we did. We finished last, but it was the first time he had ever been in a race and done everything right; a huge accomplishment, and a step in the right direction. We did the same thing the following week and finished a little closer to the rest of the field. After a few more races and some equipment changes to his bridle—limiting his vision of the other horses crowding around him at the starting gate— we were finally ready to be competitive. My boy had finally figured out how to be a real race horse and the crowd was on their feet as the misfit horse, Khaki's Fancy, and I soared down the stretch, 20 lengths ahead of the field, crossing the wire in our first win together.

We finished out the summer confidently, improving with every start, and looking forward to the following fair season. We had become an unstoppable team! The following summer, we were the ones to beat. Race after race, win after win, so many, in fact, that we were awarded the top Pacer of the Year Award! After every race, win or lose, was a phone call to Bobby Williams, eagerly waiting to hear how "his boy" had done at the track that day. To this day, I believe that Bobby was meant to have that horse come into his life, so I could meet him and have Khaki's Fancy come into mine. It just proves that anything can be achieved in the right hands.

Written by Amber Sawyer

Khaki's Fancy and I raced together on the Wisconsin County Fair circuit for nearly a decade. Our accomplishments and continued success earned us the prestigious Pacer of the Decade Award, the highest honor awarded for harness racing in the state of Wisconsin.

SUPERSTITIOUS MINDS

Bad luck, good luck, lucky charms, and myths are everywhere and the horse racing world is no different.

Perhaps the most popular myth is to hang a horseshoe upside down "so your luck doesn't run out."

Legend has it that, in the Middle Ages, a blacksmith named Dunstan was visited by The Devil, who asked him to make him some horseshoes. Dunston refused and beat the devil, making him promise to never enter a door where a horseshoe was hung upside down, capturing the devil's luck inside it.

One white foot, buy him. Two white feet, try him. Three white feet, look well about him. Four white feet, do without him. This myth came about years ago because people believed white feet were softer and more brittle than black feet. Some people also believed horses with white feet were unlucky.

No peanuts in the barn. No one knows where this belief originated, but no horseman dare to test its truth.

Never race in brand new equipment.

Never cut a horse's hair on race day! Some horsemen take this to heart and refuse to even shave on race day!

Straw left in your pitchfork is bad luck.

No pictures before the race.

A horse with tangles in its main is said to be ridden by fairies at night.

The Prophet's Thumbprint is said to be the most blessed mark a horse can bear. Some horses have a small indentation in the muscle on their neck. Legend has it that this is the mark of the Prophet Muhammad, who blessed five of his most loyal mares with his thumbprint. The story continues to say that any horse with this mark are descendants of one of these five mares and are said to be especially strong, loyal, and brave.

If it's a rainy day, bet on the gray.

After a win, keep everything the same. Same clothes all the way down to your socks, same wraps and bandages and all the same equipment on the horse.

Many tracks have no Barn number 13 on its grounds and many are labeled with letters instead of numbers for this reason.

New track, new barn, means a new broom.

The bigger the ears, the better the horse. Large ears are believed to be a sign of intelligence and good temperament.

Old horseman sit around the barn spinning tails of success, favorite horses, and days gone by. No shedrow would be complete without the warnings of superstitions and spinning of tales. Some do it for the fun, while others had habits that turned into superstitions. The human mind and Lady Luck can be fooled once in a while.

Which one of these superstitions do you believe in?

Written by Amber Sawyer

LOUIE, LOUIE

It was my first time being away from home. I was just 19 years old. My father's quiet house in the country, my bedroom window where I looked out at the stars, the moon as the only light shining in, and the lullaby of crickets singing me to sleep were over 1,000 miles away in Wisconsin.

My new apartment was in the bustling little town of Mount Joy, Pennsylvania. It was just a small town, but the bright street lights shining into my window and the constant traffic outside made it hard to sleep at night. I moved out there to pursue my passion of working for a large harness racing stable. I grew up racing the small County Fair circuit in Wisconsin, Michigan, and Illinois, but I always dreamed of setting foot on some of the most prestigious racetracks in the country.

I answered an ad for a stable in Pennsylvania looking for a groom. I packed what I could in my car and was eastbound. A few days in, I was exercising a horse on the track, crying from homesickness, when Louie came up behind me with his horse. He had a little bit of homesickness as well, for his home state of Massachusetts. We became fast friends, despite the 40-year age difference. When we weren't racing horses at night, we were out to dinner, sharing memories and stories of our pasts. Every night we were up and down the roads of the East Coast, traveling to New Jersey, Maryland, Virginia, Pennsylvania, and all over New York State. There were so many laughs and memories made.

I had the chance to travel more, and Louie and I parted ways after only a few short months. Our friendship continued states apart and, before I knew it, I was back in Wisconsin once again racing horses at the county fairs, now with a newborn son. Louie had also left the farm in Pennsylvania and had a few horses of his own, one of them being the 12-year-old stallion, Classical Laag. One day my phone rang. It was my old friend, Louie.

"The old horse isn't fast enough to compete here on the New York tracks." Would I take him to race at the fairs? And he said "If you ever decide to breed him I want to come out and drive one of his babies at the county fairs in Wisconsin."

A few weeks later, a beautiful stallion arrived at my farm. He was so well-mannered, and I had so much fun racing him at the fairs. We even raced him under saddle. And best of all, 11 months later, a sweet little bay colt was born! The mother was a tough racing mare named Lil Miss Hilkris, and, to honor my friend, I named that colt Lil Mr. Louie. When I told Louie about his new namesake, he almost cried, as if it were his own child. Louie had no children of his own, this horse was the closest thing to family he had.

Over the next few years, I called Louie once a week to keep him up to date on his namesake's progress. From breaking, to training, and finally to his very first race, Louie was as involved as if the horse was his very own. And he always said after every phone conversation, "I'm going to drive him one day." At over 70 years old, I never thought he would ever make the 1,000-mile trip. But I obliged the old man, because I knew how happy it made him feel to think about it.

One day I got a phone call. "When you enter Louie in the race this weekend, list me as the driver. I'm on a bus. I'm on my way."

When Louie got off the bus, it was the first time we'd seen each other in 12 years. We were up all night reminiscing, and the next day the pair of Louies were warming up on the track for the race at the county fair. The day we talked about for years had finally come true. Louie, in his bright pink racing gear, and Louie, in his red, white, and green racing silks approached the starting gate and it was like the years had just melted off the old man. The pair of Louies finished in third place that day, the feeble, once slow-moving 71-year-old man was no longer; just a driver out on the track, fulfilling a dream. It really wouldn't have mattered where the Louies finished that day, to finally see Louie driving his namesake after all this time was priceless. He came back to the barn. He slowly unharnessed the bay gelding, and a silence fell upon him. He was reflecting on a lifetime; almost 40 years in the sport of harness racing, and the realization had hit home. This was probably the last race he'd ever be in. He slowly unbuckled his helmet and unbuttoned his red green and white driving silks, folded them, and carefully placed them in his driving bag for the very last time, knowing they would never be put on again. It was a quiet ride back home from the track that day. The next day, Louie was back on the bus headed home, and we talked about the next time we'd be seeing each other, knowing all too well, the truth.

Rest in peace, my dear friend.

In memory of Louis O. Pasciuti
January 25, 1943—March 18, 2018

Written by Amber Sawyer

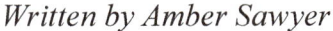

SO MUCH IN COMMON

"We never have to tell our horse that we are sad, happy,
confident, angry, or relaxed. He already knows, long before we do."
-Marjike de Jong

My owner trusted me, so many times, on so many trails. We rode together for miles. I didn't mean for her to fall off; something spooked me, and I ran for dear life. When I finally stopped running, I looked for her. My saddle was still on; the bit still in my mouth. I tried to find my way back to make sure she was okay. I felt so bad that I let her down. The Northwoods of Wisconsin at night can be a scary place. There are so many strange sounds. Coyotes howling, the rustling in the trees. What's out there? I wondered. The sky got so dark at night, except for the stars. For 10 days I kept wandering, hoping for someone to find me. My saddle was twisted and almost falling off. Finally I heard my name, "Luke!" That's me! Take me home! It felt so good to be home, but now I'm nervous and anxious, and I can tell my owner feels the same way. I didn't like the saddle slipping off of me in the woods, it pinched and hurt me inside. How can I tell her that I'm frightened now? I don't want to be bad, but I only have one way to let her know I'm uncomfortable. I want my owner to feel safe. She is going to try to find me a new home because she loves me and wants what's best for me. "Be a good boy," she tells me. I can feel that she is sad to say goodbye to me. I hope my new owners understand and listen to me. I heard someone tell the nice couple who came to look at me that I have a bucking problem and that I'm dangerous. "That's not me!" I want to tell them. I'm a little nervous about meeting them. I hope they like me and take me to live with them. Miss Morgan and her husband seem so nice. I can tell they are good people. It's snowing heavily outside and I rode in the trailer for 4 hours before we got to their farm. For the first few months, they let me relax and feel safe. Along with my new home, they also gave me a new name, Louie. Miss Morgan has a friend who gives me massages, Magna wave therapy, and medicine for my ulcers. I love my time with her. I'm finally starting to calm down and feel like myself again. My pain is gone, and I'm doing my best to let everyone know I'm better. Miss Morgan started to ride me again and every day we start to do more and more. I live at H3 Farms and lots of people come for riding lessons and to spend time with the other horses. They all seem so happy, I can feel it. I hope I get to be a part of it someday. Finally Miss Morgan brought a small boy up to me. I can feel he is nervous and scared, but I sense more feelings in him. He seems anxious, but I show him some kindness and I feel all those bad feelings in him start to get better. I have a lot in common with this boy, he feels just like I used to. More and more children come to see me, some ride me, some brush me, some pet me, and some just like to sit with me. I can sense all their feelings and troubles and I think they need me just as much as I need them.

Luken Smooth came to H3 Ranch after his former owner was thrown from him when he spooked. He was found after 10 days in the woods, still saddled and bridled, but not the same horse he once was. Now labeled a bucking horse and deemed unsafe, Morgan Hansen and her husband decided to take a chance on the paint gelding. After some time to readjust to his new settings, some ulcer medications, massage, and Magna wave therapy, Louie, 13, was back to be ridden. He eventually became part of H3 ranches Equine Assisted Learning Program, specializing in helping people with emotional distress, self-confidence, anxiety issues, and development and responsibility of life skills. The healing power of horses is an amazing thing!

As told by Morgan Hanson,
Marion, Wisconsin.

RESPECT

There isn't a racetrack in the Midwest where he hasn't left his hoof print. His name was whispered by gamblers at the betting windows, looking for a big payout. His speed was feared by his competition on the racetrack, and his legacy will forever be a part of the history books. The black Standardbred gelding, Mr Orchard Street, began racing at the prime age of two. After that fateful first trip to the starting gate, muscles rippling, heart pounding, nostrils flaring, Mr Orchard Street was just embarking on a remarkable racing career that would surpass the norm, spanning 15 years, 10 states, and 24 different racetracks. He raced at the betting tracks until his mandatory retirement at age 14, but his racing career didn't stop there. He was headed to the small, less strenuous Wisconsin County fairs. His love of racing was apparent, as he eagerly accepted his bit every morning before heading to the track for his daily workout. At the end of his 15th year, with no signs of slowing down, it was decided to give him one more year of glory. He was 16 on that record-setting day in August when he crossed the finish line ahead of his competition, who were under a driving command to keep up. The grandstands were full of fans all rooting him on. The crowd was in hysterics to be witnessing something they would never see again. The announcer, exhilarated, confessed, "In my 50 years of announcing races I've never seen a 16-year-old set foot on a racetrack, let alone had the privilege to announce one. Ladies and gentlemen, I'm pleased to present to you the nation's oldest winning racehorse, Mr. Orchard Street!" The fans erupted as the classy, old horse headed to the winner's circle. Although he still had the heart and the strength, time was beginning to catch up to him. The air that day was filled with the aroma of cotton candy, popcorn, and corn dogs from the midway, and the bells and whistles echoed through the air as happy squealing children won their prizes. The barns were filled with excited fair goers, eager to see the horses, still wide-eyed, excited, and blowing from their races; caretakers taking off harnesses, and offering them baths and cool drinks of water. The veteran pacer hung back in his stall; the love of the sport and the passion and fire of the competition still bright in his eyes, but knowing all too well that Father Time would soon be knocking on the door of his racing career. A family came into the barn, carefully reading the names of each horse on the stalls, and stopped when they saw the shiny black horse. "Mr. Orchard Street," the husband quietly greeted the old horse. "Can I help you?" Asked his trainer. The man went on to explain. "We've been watching this horse race for so many years. My family always loved going to the track to watch the races, and almost every week we went we would watch this horse race. It was something we looked forward to every week as a family." He smiled at the memory of his wife and children, lined up on the fence near the finish wire, cheering on the old black horse with the one white sock and the blaze down his nose. "We came to the fair today as a family to watch the races, and when I saw his name in the program, I couldn't believe he was still racing. I had to stop and pay my respects." To see Mr Orchard's name in bold print in the racing program, just like he had so many years ago, brought back the nostalgic feeling of watching his children grow up, and the wonderful memories he had made at the track with his family. The 16-year-old took a step forward and the gentleman gave him a pet on the nose. "Thank you for all the memories, old friend."

Mr Orchard Street crossed his last finish line on September 15th, 2018. He retired with 322 starts, 44 wins, 36 seconds, 43 thirds and just under $200,000 in earnings. He took his lifetime mark of 1:52 at the age of four. His remarkable accomplishments echoed across the nation as the oldest winning race horse at the age of 16. He was featured in the hit show, "Around the Corner with John Mcgivern," *Hoof Beats* magazine, and the USTA's Harness Racing Fan Zone. Dubbed, "Mr Longevity" for his dance with Father Time, he retired sound and healthy. He was honored after his last race in the winner's circle for his achievements with a retirement cake and a 10 pound bag of carrots waiting for him at the barn. The horseman indulged on cake and memories; Mr Orchard Street happily munched on his carrots.

Written by Amber Sawyer

GRANDPA'S PROMISE

I always wanted a horse, but they were expensive in 1973. The saddle, the bridle, the horse—all expenses too much for a 13-year-old girl to save up on her own, but, nonetheless, I wanted a horse of my very own.

Grandpa pulled me aside one afternoon. "If you save up enough money to buy yourself a horse, I will buy your saddle."

No little girl had ever been more motivated! I started babysitting for the neighbors. Every time I felt defeated, I just remembered what I was working towards. By July, I had about half of what I needed. My parents knew how hard I'd worked and offered to pay the difference. A horse was for sale a few towns away, and I didn't want to wait any longer. We picked up Lady in a borrowed stock trailer and by the time we got home, there was Grandpa, waiting for me with a brand new, leather saddle. I wrapped my arms around him. I was so happy!

Grandpa's promise warmed my heart every time I placed that saddle on Lady's back. Even years later, the saddle decorated our home and was an everyday reminder of my grandpa's love for me so many years ago.

As told by Karen Braun Lundt,
Burnett, Wisconsin,
and Stanton, Nebraska.

SECOND CHANCES, LAKOTA'S STORY

Lakota was not the same horse from the ad I saw when I was looking for a trail horse. The owner brought out a skinny, sickly, old Pinto gelding. My brain was telling me to find something younger and healthier, but my heart tugged at those dark, brown eyes— sad, but still full of life. It was that vibrant spark that I fell in love with. I rescued him that same day.

Severely dehydrated, malnourished, underweight and with a mouth full of rotting teeth, we estimated him to be nearly 30 years old. I wasn't sure if he would recover, but I wanted what time he had left to be comfortable. He was turned out with Sweet Pea, a beautiful aging mare, white as snow. He loved her dearly. There was no doubt in my mind that, if it hadn't been for her, he never would have recovered. Lakota began eagerly digging into his daily bran mash, desperate for his second chance at life. The weight and muscle slowly began to come back, and it wasn't long before he was galloping across the field with Sweet Pea. Anytime he went somewhere, he would run as fast as he possibly could. He was literally taking his second chance and running with it. The now fat, old, sassy bay pinto was feeling good and needed a job to do to keep him out of all the trouble he was causing: opening doors, untying himself, letting himself in or out of the barn. He now had the Old Man Syndrome» of, *I do what I want when I want.*

We left the farm and Sweet Pea and headed for a lesson stable. It was obvious Lakota had been ridden before, and took to his students. He could tell which riders were beginners and which were more experienced. Sometimes, I think he knew more than we did.

Everything we offered him to do, it was clear he had already done it in some point in his life. He always acted like the biggest horse there, always wanting all the attention for himself. When he was done being outside, he let himself in. When he didn't want to work anymore, he just left. His second chance at life was definitely on his terms, and no one was going to tell him otherwise. He was so patient teaching his students that we thought, *Why not try him in the show ring for the kids to learn on as well?*

He walked into the ring, and it was obvious he had done it before. His head was held high, his ears were perked, and that spark in his eye was just as bright as ever. Lakota was well into his thirties—was there no end to his accomplishments? He placed in every class he was in: halter, walk/trot, and showmanship. I thought back to the sickly, skinny, old boy I felt so sorry for. My expectations had been on the floor, and he shot them to the moon and back. Lakota had spent his second chance at life helping, teaching, and taking care of everyone that crossed his path, but the time was coming to turn the tables.

He went back to the farm after two years, and there was Sweet Pea, eagerly waiting for him. The spark was dimming in her eyes as well, but she instantly recognized the love of her life and eagerly walked up to meet him as he did his best to gallop to her. It was heartwarming. They had a beautiful summer together. I knew that Lakota would never tell me when his time was up; he was too proud for that.

My wedding was coming up in the fall, and it was so important to have them be a part of it. The photos turned out beautiful, with Romeo Lakota and his Juliet, Sweet Pea, in the background. Two star-crossed lovers nearing the end of their love story, just as I was beginning mine. Winter was fast approaching and I knew the cold weather would be difficult on them, but Lakota and Sweet Pea were so in love, I felt the right thing to do would be to put them to rest together, as soulmates, meant to be together forever.

Memory bracelets were made from their tails to keep them with me always. I wanted a photo of them for my wall next to our wedding photos. The day the photographer came out and laid Sweet Pea's bracelet on a branch, perfectly still, just as she had always been, but Lakota's lay crooked, dancing in the breeze. The photographer chuckled, "Was Lakota an active horse? Because I can't keep his bracelet still to photograph it!"

"Give it time," I said. "That's Lakota! He'll settle down when he's ready."

As told by Bonnie Lee Chapek,
Madison, Wisconsin.

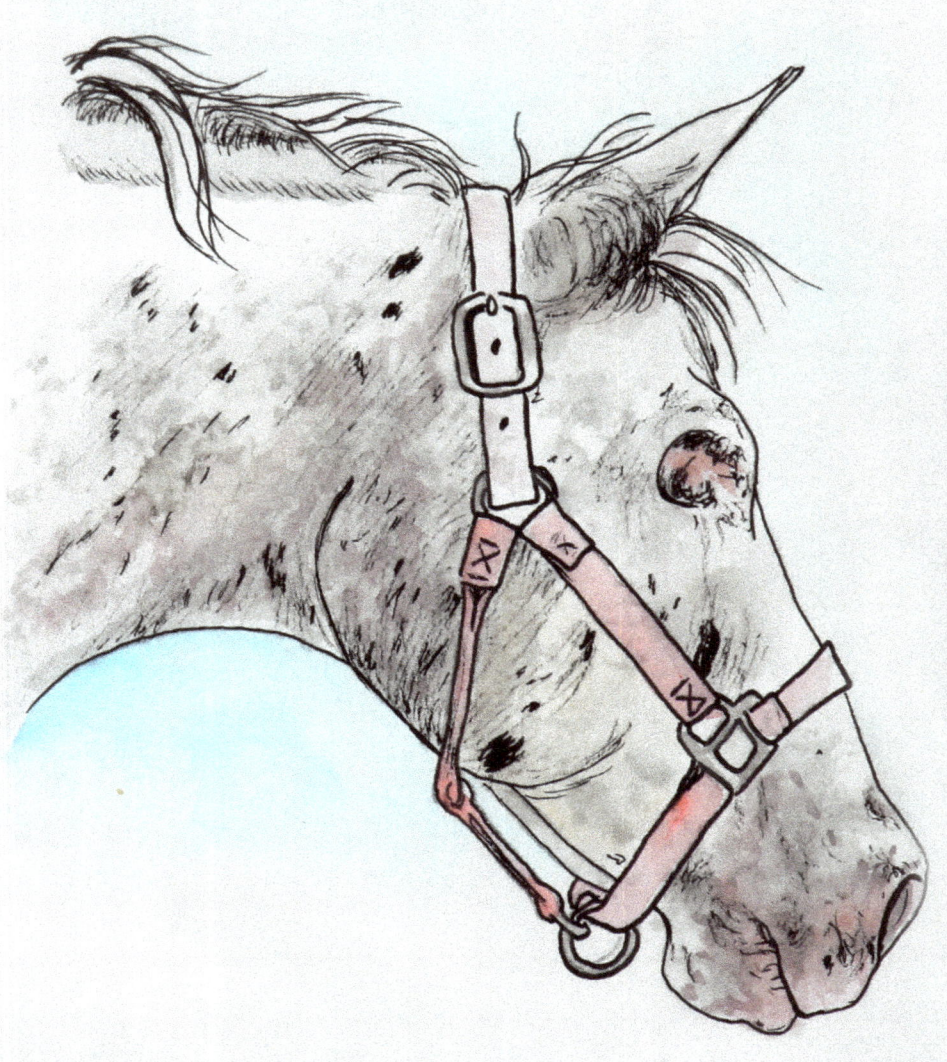

HOPE

You will see me, but I will never see you. My name is Hope. Hope is my gift to the world. It's what I have to offer. It's a big part of who I am. Hope was the strength to keep going after a horrible accident cost me my left eye. My owners tried desperately to save it, but it wasn't possible. I always enjoyed the fresh air and scenery of a relaxing trail ride. When my right eye stopped working a year later, I wondered, *How I can continue to do what I love to do when I can't see what was is in front of me?*

But I had hope. Helen Keller once said, "Blindness is an unfortunate handicap, but true vision does not require the eyes."

I was soon back out on the trail. I wasn't about to let anything stop me. I couldn't see the open fields, but I could feel the warm sun on my cream-colored coat. I couldn't see the birds flying overhead, but their chattering and singing now told me they were nearby. When we entered the woods, I couldn't see the trees around me, but I could feel the air get cooler as we trekked deeper and deeper into the forest. The crackle of branches underneath my feet told me to tread carefully. The clip clap of the pavement told me we were leaving the trail and riding the road. The soft grass told me we were on the trail, and when we made our way up the hill on the gravel, I knew we are on our way home.

I couldn't see my rider, but their hands told me if they were confident or afraid. When I became a mother, I couldn't see my sweet little baby, but I recognized her by smell, and her sweet little noises told me when she was near. I felt her warmth when she nuzzled in for a drink of warm milk.

I can smell the fresh, green grass of spring. I can taste the dry, hot air of summer. I can hear the crackle of leaves in the fall, and I can feel the coolness of the air on a crisp, wintery morning.

Someone once said, "You will see this mare, but this mare will never see you." I see you in so many different ways; some you never even thought of. I can tell if you are tall or short, light or heavy, old or young, but most importantly, just by the sound of your voice I can feel if you are kind, happy, sad, or something is troubling you. I have been given all these gifts. Maya Angelou said it best, "We are only as blind as we want to be."

As told by Elizabeth Jones,
Dodgeville, Wisconsin.

This was a difficult story for me to write. I was having trouble with the best way to share Hope's story. Her owners were gracious enough to let me come to Dodgeville, Wisconsin, to ride her. While we were on the trail, instead of watching my surroundings, I closed my eyes and felt the world the way Hope experiences it. She is an amazing mare, and it was one of the great privileges of my life for her to share her world with me.

- Amber

JUST A BROWN HORSE

Sorrel. Umber. Mahogany. Tan. Chocolate. Tawny. Bronze. Russet. Cinnamon. Henna. Cocoa. Dun. Coffee. Taupe. Rust. Brunette. Neutral. Burnt. No matter how many ways you dress up the word, it's just a fancy way to say "brown."

He was just a brown, grade, quarter horse mix in an auction pen in the small town of Kalona, Iowa, a town with less than 3,000 people.

Thousands of brown horses just like him go through the auction block every week, as eager buyers sit around the sales ring, paddle in hand, nibbling on a piece of freshly made Amish cherry pie, waiting for a deal.

When the plain, old, brown gelding, with two white feet and a star, and just under 15 hands took his turn in the ring, very few paddles went up to bid on him. He was shaggy and thin, with no papers, blind in one eye, and a little off in his left hind leg. He was most likely headed for slaughter, an ugly truth for many.

Becky Peterson and her mom were looking for a horse for her 6-year-old son. The gavel of the auctioneer went down at $525 on the plain, old, brown horse. The old horseman saying goes, "One white foot, try them. Two white feet, buy them. Three white feet, be on the sly. Four white feet, pass him by."

The trio made their way home, just under a 200-mile trip to a small town in southwest Wisconsin. They named the plain, old, brown horse Clyde and, after unloading him off the trailer, introduced him to Becky's 6-year-old son, Rylan, who was terrified of horses at the time. Becky couldn't help but chuckle at the sight of the two of them slowly getting to know each other, as she had told herself so many times that she never wanted to own a brown horse; there were just so many of them out there.

Clyde quickly took to his young friend, and they were soon riding together. There was something about Clyde's gentle nature that brought young Rylan out of his shell. The Mill Creek Saddle Club was hosting Gymkhana events, and young Rylan, now seven, was eager to participate. The gentle, brown gelding gingerly took his still timid rider around the barrels and poles, and, by the end of the day, they were proudly showing off their fourth-place buckle.

Rylan proudly rode his plain, old, brown horse again the following summer, now with even more confidence. Becky's middle daughter, at 5 years old, took the plain, old, brown horse to a few speed shows the following year; and Clyde, as always, gave his rider everything she needed.

The next rider will be Becky's youngest son, soon to be three, to ride the plain, old, brown horse, and Clyde, of course, will oblige.

Becky thinks back to that auction barn in that small Iowa town where she thought she was just buying a plain, old, brown horse. "He might not have been anything special to anyone else, but he's pretty special to us."

As told by Becky Peterson, Boaz, Wisconsin.

HOT SHOT

Picture it: 1979. A postage stamp was 15 cents. Gas was only 88 cents a gallon. Jimmy Carter was President of the United States, everyone was listening to the hit song "My Sharona," by The Knack, and Michelle Peterson fell in love with her Palomino quarter horse, 9-year-old Hot Shot.

"Hot Shot was my everything; my first horse, my first love, and my refuge after a rough day of high school." Michelle reminisced. "He was my best friend."

For 3 years she rode him in open shows. They were as close as two could get. "I needed him more than ever when my parents were getting divorced."

She would wrap her arms around his neck, and he would nuzzle her to let her know he would be there for her, no matter what. And then one day, he was gone. "My parents sold him out from under me."

Michelle was heartbroken, and vowed that no other horse could replace Hot Shot; her horse days were over. The years flew by—as they tend to do. Michelle was married with three small girls. A stay at home mom, she was looking for an outlet and convinced her husband to build a barn on their property. He immediately said *yes*, and she began the search for a horse for riding lessons at their farm. The last nail had been set and the paint was drying on that beautiful, sunny day, when the phone rang. The voice on the other line was unfamiliar.

"Hello?" the caller said. "My name is Juanita. You don't know me, but I have something that belongs to you." It was Hot Shot! My boy! Juanita's health was failing and she felt it was only right to track down the original owner of the horse she had bought 18 years ago. Michelle went to see him and he instantly remembered her. "There's no better place I'd love to see him than with you," Juanita said.

Now 27 years old, Hot Shot was delivered to his forever home with Michelle, her husband, and their three girls. Michelle noticed something strange on her gelding's papers. First, she was still listed as the owner; the papers had never been changed. Second was the date she purchased him so many years ago: July 29th, 1979. She looked at the date on the calendar: July 29th, 1997. It was exactly 18 years to the day that Hot Shot returned to her!

Michelle's first horse also became her girls' first horse. "Seeing them on his back enjoying him as much as I did is the greatest gift that I could ever have imagined." She reflected, "We had six great years of loving him before he passed, with his head on my lap."

Sometimes when you lose something and it comes back to you, it was meant to be. Michelle now operates Copper Door Farms, an Equine Guided Therapy Farm in Antioch, Illinois.

Horses have come and gone since him, but there will never be another Hot Shot.

As told by Michelle Peterson,
Antioch, Illinois.

WRITTEN IN THE STARS

"A world without horses is like a sky without stars."

For 11 years, I had given all my love to my horse, Justin. When he left us, I was broken and devastated. He was the horse that had given me all the love he had to give. To honor his memory, I wanted to give all my love to a horse that was down on his luck; one that was misunderstood and, most importantly, one that needed me almost as much as I needed him.

I was in Illinois sitting in my car on a starlit night, staring at the heavens. Looking at the constellations always helps to calm me and guide me. Orion's Belt was particularly bright in the sky that night as I was searching the auction sights looking for my new best friend. There he was, in a kill pen in Texas; a horse as bright white as the three stars on the great hunter's belt that night. His rescue price was only $875. The ad was simple: *Broke, gentle, Oklahoma-foaled, 15 hands.*

I liked his confirmation, and I've always loved white horses. He was the perfect size to pursue my passion to play polo. I bought him immediately, still sitting in my car, without a moment's hesitation. I named him before I even laid eyes on him in person: "Orion," my favorite constellation, and Greek for "Heaven's light." I made arrangements to get him to a friend's farm in Oklahoma, where I'm originally from, for quarantine. He was a little too much for my friend to handle, so I sent him to the University of Oklahoma for some training with their polo team. That's when I found the ad had been completely misleading. He had been a loose-pen auction horse, unwilling to be caught, not broke at all, and definitely not the white, gentle beauty I had hoped for. Who knew how many pens this horse had bounced around before ending up with me?

The University didn't want to deal with him, so I had no choice but to find a way to get him home to Illinois. I found a cheap trailer online. It had belonged to a rodeo queen; full of bright, shiny lettering and glitter. Dad and I hauled him home in a 1990 Chevy Blazer and a rhinestone trailer. We must have been quite a site with all the heads we turned rolling down the highway! Orion didn't like to be touched, was afraid of everyone, and wanted nothing to do with a saddle. Everything seemed to be going wrong! I sent him to a jousting trainer for 60 days, but shortly after, the COVID-19 pandemic was in full swing. I had no job, a crazy horse, and the worst case of anxiety I'd ever experienced in my life from trying to deal with him. I pushed through it. I had nothing else to do but to go to the barn every day. I stayed and worked with him as long as I was able to, and that became our everyday routine. Week after week, we were able to do a little more together.

The repetition was doing us both some good, and finally, by the end of the year, I felt we had enough work under our belts to attend a polo practice, where we practiced some stick and ball on the field with the other horses. By the spring of 2021, one of the regular polo players volunteered to try Orion in a match. They played their first match together, and he liked Orion immediately.

They played together throughout that summer, and finally I felt comfortable enough to play on him. We played our first full tournament in the fall of 2022, and he just kept getting better! He was welcomed back at Oklahoma State University's Polo team that fall. With polo on hold for the winter, I didn't want him to forget everything he learned. We were going to get ready for the prestigious Kalloway Tournament, the biggest event in polo, that fall! Three years of hard work paid off when our team took first place! It was our biggest accomplishment yet, but we still had one more goal to achieve: to play polo in our home state of Oklahoma. When I found out that Orion was also originally from Oklahoma as well, I thought the best thing we would do together would be to go back to our roots and accomplish that together after how far we'd come.

Shortly before we were set to leave, Orion fell and scraped his knee. I wanted to make sure he was okay before we made the 12-hour trip to the Sooner State. The vet took an X-ray just to be sure he was all right, but when the picture came up, my jaw dropped! Just below his knee was a small, barely noticeable Derringer bullet! No one had ever caught it. He'd been bounced around the auction pen for so long that it went unnoticed. All of my questions over the last three years were answered with that one black and white image. This horse wasn't nasty or mean, or unwilling. He was afraid and untrusting; and had been in pain. All this time, he had been trying to tell everyone in the best way he knew how. And to think, I was ready to give up on him too, but I remembered why I got him in the first place; to give my love to someone who needed me most. I'll never know how he got that bullet or when it happened. All I know is this beautiful, patient, loving, and trusting animal has taught me one of the most important lessons: "Never give up on the ones that need you the most."

SMALL AND MIGHTY SOPHIE

Shakespeare once said, "And though she be but little, she is fierce." In his classic play, "A Midsummer Night's Dream," Helena was referring to her friend Hermia as a force to be reckoned with (Act 3, Scene 2).

Shakespeare clearly had never met little Sophie, the Mustang quarter pony. She stands only 13 hands, but she doesn't know it. Kathy Neff was looking for a horse for her daughter, Grace, but little Sophie's personality proved to be a little too big for her. She needed a little patience and gentling before she could be ridden, but when Kathy's daughter entered junior high school, the little pony made the perfect partner. She could rope, cut cattle, run barrels, goat tie, break away, and pole bending.

There was no limit to what she could do. "We got Sophie when she was seven." Kathy said. "Her past was a mystery. She was too high strung when we got her, it took her some time to settle down."

Sophie took a while to put her faith in people, but once she did, that bond was unbreakable. There was no end to "the little mare that could." Sophie›s resume expanded to trail rides, pulling a sled, and jumping. It was obvious that someone from her past had taught her well. She even qualified for the Junior High Nationals for barrel racing! The smaller the arena; the bigger advantage she had against the other horses, who were much larger than her. All the kids wanted a chance to compete with fierce little Sophie, who also mastered pole bending!

"When she's at a show, she just knows her job," Kathy said. "She's the handy little horse that gets used wherever she's needed. She doesn't even notice that the other horses tower over her, she just loves the excitement!"

At 22 years old, in 2024, Sophie has decided she has no plans for retirement. The stubborn little mare whinnied at the fence after almost being left behind on Kathy's way to a competition.

"Wait for me!" She demanded!

"All right Sophie," Kathy gave in. "You can come along, get in the trailer!"

"Patience in love can do wonders for a horse."
- Kathy Neff

As told by Kathy Neff,
Gratiot, Wisconsin.

A HORSE'S LIFE ON RACE DAY

In her country, Keisha was the youngest jockey. She had a Thoroughbred named Skie. She used him for racing. She had been to six races before and she said this was the biggest race of her life. She was going to the Petta World Cup. She got there and went in the trailer, got on her silks, and tacked up her horse. After she warmed up, she went to the race course: it was so big! She went into the gate stalls and the intro dude said, "And they're OFF!" Keisha's heartbeat went off for second and back on. She easily went in front of the others, but there was one rider she could not catch up to, but she successfully did and fell off!

CHAPTER 2: OFF TO THE HOSPITAL

The paramedics rushed over when she was out of shock. She asked, "IS MY HORSE OKAY?" They replied, "Yes, someone tamed it and brought it back to your trailer. I think it was your trainer. Anyway, let's get you to the hospital." Keisha's mother and father came to see her, she had seven stitches on her head. Her mother said, "Seven's a lucky number." They both laughed. A few days later, she was ready to race. The end!

This story was written and stapled together to make a book and gifted to me by an 8 year-old girl from Connecticut. One of my favorite things about being an author is inspiring young authors, and I always love the gifts of stories they have written for me. This story has not been altered in anyway; these were her exact words and illustrations.

- Amber

biggest race in her life shes going to the Petta World cup.

sucsesfully did and fell

DOUBLE DUTY

W e've had a lot of wins with him, but this win was, by far, the best." Shane Taggart wasn't talking about a trip to the winner's circle with their Standardbred gelding, King Otra, but the blue ribbon their 6-year-old daughter, Madison, would be taking home after she and the family racehorse won their halter class at the Cumberland County Riding Club in Cumberland, Maine. The son of Western Ideal out of the Artsplace mare, Queen Otra, had just raced at Scarborough Downs harness racing track in Southern Maine, the day before. Mady's mother, Amy, couldn't be more proud of their daughter.

"She loves horses. She's always at the barn with us, and King is hardly ever in his stall." Mady is usually out leading him around, and King, loving every minute of it, is following her around like a puppy.

The thought of showing him had never crossed her mind until, during one of Mady and King's daily strolls, a fellow horseman suggested to Amy that they enter the upcoming halter show at the local riding club. "We were a nervous wreck at that first show," Amy chuckled at the memory of August 2018. "My husband, Shane, stood in the ring with Mady, probably more for his own comfort than hers." But King was the perfect gentleman. After a few more shows that year, and even more the following year, the winner of $409,000 in his racing career was also racking up the ribbons at his side job as a show horse. Sometimes the old horse would show up in the racing barn, perfectly polished with glitter still in his hair, from the show the evening before. Shane, as his driver, would come off the racetrack with his silks dusted in glitter. A breed known for their versatility and willingness to adapt and learn new things, King Otra is the epitome of Standardbreds.

"He may not have been the fastest," Amy admitted, "but he's always come through for us, whether it was on the racetrack or in the showring." He's proven himself as the horse that just keeps giving, and perhaps, King has given so much because of the pure, beautiful love he's been gifted in return. After all, every horse deserves to be loved by a little girl.

As told by Amy Taggart,
Monticello, New York

ANGELS EVERYWHERE

There's a magical place tucked away in a sleepy little town in Southeast Wisconsin. It's a 160 year-old village where miracles happen and angels appear. Less than 3,000 people call home to the town where faith is restored and animals and people work together to heal each other. In their own backyard, there's a phenomenon similar to a church where all are welcome and no one is turned away. The world is blessed to have a woman named Marianne Shulz. Even at a young age, she always believed that animals were a gift from God. Any injured animal she found would find itself a home at their family farm.

God's work continued through her years later when she founded Riding With Angels on 50 acres of land in Palmyra, Wisconsin. She had no idea the journey she was about to begin, the lives she would change, or potentially save, and the influence she would have on so many people, whom, without her, would never have been touched by the healing power of horses.

Marianne did her best to rescue any animal that needed her: horses, alpacas, goats, and even a zebra. She had a dream that her place would always be a safe place for people to bring their horses that they were no longer able to care for, and a refuge for those in need of a soft mane to brush, a warm neck to cry in, an ever-listening ear, and an eager muzzle to take a treat.

The four-legged weren't the only ones in need of rescuing. Less than an hour away, in the inner city of Milwaukee, in the smog, graffiti, car horns, gunshots, and the dirty streets, there were plenty of kids in need of rescuing as well, but for different reasons. These were victims of the unimaginable: the neglected, the gang members, the abused, the abandoned, and the discarded. Marianne, with her ever-giving nature, reached out to these children, who often sought refuge from the streets at the local community center. *Who better to heal and comfort these children than horses with the same background*, she thought? There's no better one to heal than one who has been through the same.

Marianne wanted to share her blessings with those less fortunate, and began inviting kids from the center to her farm. It was difficult at first for some of the kids who lived by no one's rules but their own. The farm was an entirely different way of life than they had ever seen. The rough and tough gang members who were raised on the streets with the "tough as nails" attitude quickly melted down at the overpowering size of a 1200 pound horse in front of them, and swiftly grew meek knowing this animal was not intimidated. The fact that these horses were outcasts, just like them, brought them together.

Here, they were asked about their dreams, their hopes, and their plans for the future—something most of them had never given a second thought to—and their eyes lit up at the thought that someone believed in them and wanted to hear their life's ambitions. For many of them, their sights laid no further than where their next meal would come from. It was a comfort knowing that they would leave Riding With Angels with a hot meal in their bellies.

As more and more children visited Marianne's farm, the miracles began to multiply. Nick was a popular horse among the kids at the farm. As an ex-carriage horse, he was skinny and malnourished before being rescued. So many of the kids remember seeing him on the streets of Milwaukee, and it was easy to relate to someone who came from the same background as they did. His big heart and love for life connected with those feeling down on themselves and their future. A 30-year-old mare was gifted to Riding With Angels and continued to live the rest of her life feeling loved and appreciated. As Marianne believes, "All life has value."

Two draft horses, Babe and Silver, found their home in Marianne's care. As a team, Babe had always been the lazier of the two, leaving most of the work for Silver. When Silver went blind, the roles reversed and it was Babe who carried the workload for her companion, being her eyes and caregiver. In Silver's final days, Babe was by her side and comforted her until she passed. The old horse stood watch over her grave for 4 days, mourning her partner of 23 years. Was it an act of Divine intervention that nudged Babe into reversing rolls with her partner?

We'll never know what caused the transformation, but another alteration took place at Riding With Angels, which proved the existence of miracles on that small Palmyra farm. Mary Ann told the story. "We had a girl who volunteered at our farm from a very well-to-do family, with an attitude to match. Helping the less fortunate seemed beneath her, until she met a girl from the program who had been through the unspeakable. The two girls from different backgrounds grew closer, and that Christmas, instead of asking for gifts for herself, she asked her family for donations to help the girl and those less fortunate."

Another child rarely spoke before coming to the farm. During her visits, she would find her favorite horse and curry comb, and whisper ever so quietly to the horse, who was listening contently. Only God knows the conversations that went on between that girl and her horse.

Isaiah 36:6 tells us, "Then the lame will leap like a deer, and the mute tongue will shout for joy." The Bible verse held true then and still to this day of the miracles that are among us. Perhaps His greatest miracle came in the form of a young gang member who had spent most of his short life on the streets of Milwaukee. After two years of feeling a part of something special at Riding With Angels and believing his life had value, he became a pastor.

There is no end to the number of miraculous stories to come out of that rustic small town, tucked away in that Southeastern corner of Wisconsin. Riding With Angels was named on the belief that angels are all around us, as gift sent to us from God. But He also sent us an angel named Marianne.

As told by Marianne Schulz,
Palmyra, Wisconsin.

THE LETTER

Skipper Boy, the big, black, beautiful gelding was by far the most stunning horse I'd ever seen. And the best part was, he was all mine. I was only 16 years old when I bought Skipper, just a young kid looking for a start in the harness racing business and taking a gamble on my very first racehorse. I think back to my first drive, approaching the starting gate with my boy, donning my signature red silks. I will never forget the exhilarating feeling of the horses taking their position behind the starting car, with nostrils flaring, sweat flying off of rippling muscles, the hum of sulky tires, and the powerful thunder of hooves vying for position when the starter said "GO!"

Skipper taught me more in the two minutes of that race than I ever could have learned from any book. The unfortunate part of the business is that we can't keep all the horses we fall in love with. Life and adulthood started to catch up with me. Standardbred racehorses are bred to work; it's what they love and it's who they are, so I sold my beautiful Skipper Boy to a reputable Amish gentleman from outside of town. And that was it, my favorite horse was just a memory.

Life went on and Skipper was frequently on my mind. I often wondered, *Was he happy? Was he well taken care of?* There were other horses, but none could replace my Skipper Boy.

One day, out of nowhere, the most unexpected thing happened. In the mailbox that day was a letter, hand-addressed to me. I opened it up, hands shaking, seeing the return address. Two pages of praises on my Skipper Boy! He had ended up in loving hands, the pride of his owner. He was the driving horse every gentleman dreamed of and turned every head on his way to church each Sunday. His sleek, black coat matched the equally polished, sleek, black buggy, as he proudly carried his new family to worship services each Sunday. My heart fluttered as I imagined my boy, making his new family as happy as he had made me. It was destiny that he ended up in that loving home. With tears welling up in my eyes, I gingerly folded up that letter.

Skipper Boy, a foal of 1980, bankrolled $35,328 in his racing career that spanned 7 years. He took his lifetime mark of 1:59.3 on a half-mile track at the age of 6. He retired from the racetrack on October 12, 1989 at Saratoga Raceway, located in Saratoga Springs, New York.

Greg Decker Jr.'s very first drive on Skipper Boy at the age of 16 was merely the beginning of a career that has spanned 3 5 years and an impressive $1,000,000 in purses. 3,940 drives later, he has won 448 races, 559 seconds, and 615 thirds. Every time he picks up his driving lines, Skipper Boy crosses his mind; and their journey together so long ago.

As told by Greg Decker Jr.
Monticello, New York.

A GHOST STORY

Never judge someone based on where they come from. You never know if they need you, or if you need them, or if you need each other. The bright, red horse barn was torn down, saddles and shiny bridles sold off, the smell of fresh hay and pasture no longer filled the air, and the gentle echo of a horse's knicker and soft whinny faded on the breeze. Emmie Crotteau was a firm believer in faith, but in the last eight months her faith in everything had been tested. Her father passed away, she suffered a devastating miscarriage, and her paint horse, Moon, was lost to cancer. Never again would she own another horse, she told herself over and over again, as she packed up the last of the brushes, horseshoes, and curry combs.

Emmie threw herself into helping others to help herself heal from her own losses in the healthcare industry. Mindlessly scrolling the internet after a long tiresome day, she stopped suddenly and looked down at her screen as a picture of a gray horse jumped out in front of her. He was nothing but a number, 025, but something told her that she had to buy him. And without a moment's hesitation, he was hers.

Was it Divine intervention? A sign from a higher power? Whatever it was, she put her faith in that sad, gray horse who was all the way in Texas, but she believed that it was meant to be, and her new horse would make his way to her safely. Her faith was again tested as multiple mishaps delayed the shipment: quarantine, illness; it seemed like he would never get to her. It was 1 o'clock in the morning almost 3 months later when Emmie's gray stepped off the trailer, and she finally laid eyes on her new project. He looked almost ghostly in the moonlight, with the stars reflecting off his ashen coat. His name stuck. Ghost and Emmie had a long road to recovery. Her faith got him there, his faith in her was to be determined if he was a survivor.

He had a rough road ahead.

Their best guess was that, at nearly 17 hands and all legs, he was mostly Thoroughbred and around 20 years-old. One thing was for certain, Ghost had terrible teeth, bite marks, barbed wire scars, and didn't like to be touched. Number 025 had bounced around so much, it was no wonder he had trust issues, but his eyes said to Emmie that he knew she would heal him. Her challenge was to figure out how. And so their journey began. Ghost had a dedicated team to help him through his fight. A nutritionist, his vet, Emmie, and her best friend, Bonnie, were all on his side. The rest was up to Ghost.

Emmie was looking for answers anywhere she could find them. She came across a woman named Julez, an animal communicator, to help her read her four-legged friend. Julez had always been able to read the energy of animals, even at a young age. At first she called it a curse; seeing spirits and constantly hearing more of the world around her than the average person. She harnessed her gift and became certified in holistic healing, and practices Araki healing, using the energy of the universe. One of her miraculous healing stories goes back to the day she found a horse trapped in the woods. "I kept hearing a voice, a kind of energy, telling me there was something out there begging for help."

She can't explain her gift, but best describes it as a puzzle piece, and she has to fix the puzzle. Ghost told her that he had often been mistreated and misunderstood previously. Everyone had treated him like a machine and he had lost hope by the time Emmie had come into his life. Julez believes in loving the horse first and the sport second. The best way for Emmie and Ghost to start was at the beginning: Groundwork. The old boy needed to learn how to trust again. Every time he took a step in the right direction, something would push him two steps back. He had tooth and sinus issues, ulcers, and cellulitis, but through it all Ghost was overcoming his trust issues and developing into a riding and dressage horse thanks to Emmie's longtime friend, Bonnie. But health issues were still hindering him.

Emmie decided to take matters into her own hands. She always believed that natural healing was the best way, and with her background in healthcare, she looked into body work to help her silvery friend. Ghost responded well, as Emmie dedicated nine months of her life to her certification, including a trip to an in-person class in Texas, to help him. He was a different horse. The frightened, wide-eyed, ghostly gelding from before was now a curious, people-loving, and sometimes even mischievous boy. Now known for his antics of opening doors, stealing hay, and performing mouth tricks for food, it was hard to believe it was the same horse that arrived in the dead of night that cold, late-fall day. Ghost was enjoying the trail rides and all the visitors who came, sometimes just to sit with him. His calming nature reflected on those who needed it most. Emmie saw the reaction her body work schooling had on Ghost and decided to start her own business to help other horses. She named it On Point Equine Massage and Body Work, and used Ghost's silhouette and the Bethel Star as her logo. The star, symbolizing her journey of always having to be 'on point' with Ghost and represented her faith, which brought her to him that memorable day just a few years prior. In that short period of time, he healed her, she healed him, and their friendship became an unbreakable bond.

Emmie's advice to the world is simple, "Never judge anyone off of where they came from, because they could end up being your best friend," and, most importantly, "have faith."

As told by Emmie Crotteau,
Rice Lake, Wisconsin.

THE ARTIST

"No heaven can heaven be, if my horse isn't there to welcome me."
- Author unknown.

Do you ever notice that flash of color across the skies at sunset or the bright, full rainbow after the storm has passed? There's a familiar quote that says, "No one paints like God." Spring in Wisconsin can seem never-ending. Between the sporadic blizzards, the rain, the snow thawing, and all the mud, people stare out their windows and look for brighter days ahead. Some set puzzles, some play cards or plan their summer gardens, some catch up on their favorite soap operas or TV shows, but in a small town in Dodge County, in Southeast Wisconsin, one woman taught her horse to paint.

"Horses get restless, just like people do," Carol Jensen explained. "My quarter horse, Buggs, had the energy of a three year old toddler and muddy spring days in his stall were the perfect excuse for him to try and get into trouble." Carol came across a video of a woman in Florida who had taught her horse to paint and instantly thought of Buggs. "He was so intelligent and always up for a challenge, there wasn't a doubt in my mind that I could teach him to paint." She encouraged the gelding to hold a brush in his mouth. One of his many tricks was to shake his head up and down on command, and Buggs, highly motivated by food, was always eager to learn. "Every time he did what I wanted, he got a treat, so he quickly caught on." Carol, who is an artist herself, chuckled. When Buggs perfected his painting motion, Carol began adding paint to the brushes and holding up the paper for him to create his artwork. He understood exactly what he was supposed to do, but sometimes, the rambunctious

Picasso would rip through the paper. Carol decided to upgrade the budding artist to canvas. Her ambition was to have a gallery full of his artwork. The dream became a reality when Buggs' artwork was displayed in a nearby cafe. Next to the paintings were photos of the four-legged painter in action. No one believed they were painted by a horse! Word of the local Mo'neigh" spread and it wasn't long before the papers caught wind of the local celebrity. Word quickly spread and Carol was overwhelmed with phone calls, news reporters, and radio interviews. The small town of Iron Ridge was known nationwide. The small farm had frequent visitors, hoping to catch a glimpse of the artist at work, with Carol adding fresh paint to a new brush to hand to her protégé. In all, Buggs completed over 100 paintings, more than some professional painters ever dream of. Some were sold all over the country. A few were auctioned off at a charity auction for Carol's favorite therapeutic riding stable. The most memorable sales were by Carol's friend in England, who bought several to hang in her home. She introduced Carol to a friend of hers in Wales, and the two became fast friends. Carol has even made the trip to visit several times, a long way from her home in that small Wisconsin town. "All the people I've met, experiences I've had, special memories I've made; I owe it all to Buggs. He opened so many doors for me." Carol beamed. "He was my one in a million, always up for anything and everything. He was always ready for our next adventure." Her eyes welled up with tears when she took herself back to the morning she found him standing in the pasture, head down, ears back; definitely not himself. She knew right away it wasn't good. Frantically trying to reach a vet, but it was too late, he was gone. Buggs was buried on the farm where he made so many memories. The sunset that night was more vibrant than usual. It flamed across the skies with shades of pinks, reds, oranges, yellows, and colors that haven't even been invented yet. They say, "No one paints like God" but I think from time to time, He hands the brush over to Buggs.

As told by Carol Jensen,
Iron Ridge, Wisconsin.

LIFE LESSONS

A good horse will teach you. A great horse will challenge you. Only the best will inspire you! As I sat there, watching my heart horse fade away, my teenage mind was trying to comprehend why. Fame, my Arabian, was only 8 years old, but he was fading quickly before my eyes. When the vet decided it was best to end his pain and suffering, I didn't think I would ever find another soulmate again. And then there was 4-year-old Nuberry, patiently waiting for me in the barn. He had only been with my family a few short months and we hadn't had much time to form a real connection yet, but I buried my face in his mane, and he stood there, comforting me as best as he knew how, for as long as I needed him to. If it hadn't been for that, I don't think I ever would have gotten over the tragedy of seeing my best friend slowly leaving me. Not a day went by that I didn't miss him, but Nuberry helped to ease that pain. He was with me through the highs and lows and through the ups and downs. He even went away with me to college. I attended Williams Woods University Equestrian College in Missouri. After a rough day of classes, there was Nuberry waiting to hear all about my day. After graduating, I worked three jobs to support him and myself. He taught me that horses aren't cheap and the value and reward of hard work. I had him all through my twenties, he got me through all of the ups and downs of life and all the bumps in the road. He taught me so much. Now in my 30s, we have done it all. Arabian horse shows all over the Midwest, Arabian Nationals in New Mexico, local open shows, distance riding, western, hunt, sport horse, native costume, and jumping. A few memories that stand out are our ride through the Mark Twain National Forest and our award for the Wisconsin Arabian Horse Ambassador in 2024. But nothing is more rewarding than now, in my 30s, being able to see my three children enjoy and learn from the horse that I have loved nearly half my life. Having Nuberry in my life for almost 20 years has inspired me to start my own business teaching kids about horses. He's taught riders from 2 years old to 60. My goal was to build a life that I could walk out my front door every morning and see him. If it hadn't been for God putting him in my life so many years ago, who knows where I'd be now. Newberry taught me the value of hard work, challenged me to keep looking ahead, no matter what how many difficulties life gives you, and inspired me to teach others just how wonderful it can be to be loved by a horse.

As told by Jessica Clare Horning, Madison, Wisconsin.

AGE IS JUST A NUMBER

*"There is something about the outside of a
horse that is good for the inside of a man."*
–Winston Churchill.

The year was 1966. A postage stamp was five cents, and gas was a mere thirty one cents per gallon. Lyndon B Johnson was President of the United States and "California Dreamin'" by The Mamas and the Papas was the No. 1 hit on the radio. It was also the year a then-29-year-old Robert Nadeau first slipped his hands into a set of leather hand holds and swung his leg over the seat of a wooden jog cart for the very first time. That was the moment he caught the racehorse fever.

It all started in the barn of Sheridan Smith, in Farmington, Maine. Nadeau had a background in finance but was an avid railbird, often stopping by the track on his way home from the office to watch a few races from the grandstand. By a chance encounter, Nadeau met Smith one day during the races. The two men got to talking, as horsemen traditionally do. "He invited me down to his barn to meet a horse named Billfold," Nadeau recalled. "He wasn't racing at the time, and no one in the barn really got along with him." Every one said he was no good. "Smith put me on a jog cart and sent me out to the track with him," Nadeau continued. "When I got back to the barn, Smith jokingly said, 'for $100 you can have him!'" No hundred dollar bill had ever left a man's pocket faster.

Nadeau started feeding horses at the barn in the morning and taking care of Billfold, a gelding Standardbred. The pair made their first start that summer on the Maine fair circuit. "My first win came the following year at Skowhegan Fair (Maine),"

said Nadeau. "Billfold crossed the wire in a blistering 2.13.1."
Ironically, Billfold's final race, in 1974, was in Farmington, where
the two had first met. Nadeau, who has since driven winners of 167
races, has also dabbled in the breeding business. A few broodmares
passed through his barn, but B. Direct Duncan, by Sampson
Direct, produced his most memorable foal. "Stephanie Direct, by
Stephan O, definitely taught me just as much—if not more—than
I taught her," Nadeau said. They must have done something right:
Stephanie Direct and Nadeau won their first qualifier together, and
they traveled to all of the Maine Sire Stakes races in the 1985
season. "I loved that horse," Nadeau said. And rightfully so, as
Stephanie Direct raced until she was 12 years old, earning $48,086
and taking her lifetime mark of 2:00.3 at Scarborough Downs, in
Scarborough, Maine. Nadeau's green and white colors have long
been a common sight at tracks all over New England-many now
that are just a memories without a hoof print in sight. "Lewiston,
Scarborough, the half mile track at Rockingham, Farmington-you
name it, I've been there!" Nadeau said. "I've won at every fair
track in Maine. I've always loved racing horses in Maine and New
England."

A self-taught horseman, Nadeau knew that he didn't have enough
talent to pursue a full time career in harness racing, but he still
craves the thrill of competition. "I've always had my own business
and worked full-time," Nadeau said. "I've always done everything
myself: my own training, driving, shipping, and even the shoeing.
I don't believe in doing all the work and letting someone else have
all the fun." Despite getting out of the business a few times, Nadeau
always found his way back. Over the years, the longtime resident
of Saco, Maine, has been associated with 35 horses, one of his most
memorable being the silvery Putmans Storm, lovingly nicknamed
"Putty." After bouncing through 4 different owners in 2021, he finally
found his sweet spot with the equally, ashen haired, Nadeau. "He's so
nice to drive in a race, nice to be around, and great to ship," Nadeau
said, adding that Putty wears simple racing equipment, just the bare
essentials of an open bridle, a hood with cups, his pacing hobbles, and

the protective knee and tendon boots. The duo, who participated in the Maine Amateur Driving Club last summer, share a history of lighting up the tote board in their three seasons together.

On November 17, 2021, Nadeau steered the then 12 year old Putmans Storm to a victory at Cumberland Raceway (Cumberland, Maine) and paid a staggering $63.20 to win on a $2 ticket! Only 32 days later, it was another flash of green and white silks crossing the finish line first again, just eight days before his 84th birthday. What a wonderful present from his beloved gray horse! In 2023, the two veterans reached a very special milestone that will be hard for anyone to beat. It was a beautiful summer day in June when the dynamic duet, at ages 85 and 14, respectively, logged another victory with almost a combined century between the two of them! Putnam Storm drew the rail position in a Maine Amateur Driving Club race at Cumberland Raceway that day. Nadeau determinedly left the starting car at the word GO and never looked back. The young guns of the track, 50 years his junior, tried to sneak past him after a slow half mile, but the gray horse found another gear from deep down inside his 14 year old heart, and by the 3/8th pole, there was no stopping them. The track announcer, Scott Ehrlich, not believing what he was witnessing, had Cumberland fans in a frenzy. "The combined age of your leader, Putmans Storm, and his pilot, Robert Nadeau, is a mere 99 years." Most of the excited fans with winning tickets clenched in their hands had no idea how rare this occasion was to see a horse and driver with a combined age of almost a century, was something they'd probably never be privileged to see again. Harness racing horses must retire from pari-mutuel (betting) races when they turn 15. A few weeks before his 15th birthday, the ghostly grey, Putmans Storm, was harnessed and led to the race paddock for the very last time. His final race of his career was a winning one, as he and Nadeau took the Frosty Final at Cumberland Raceway. It was the perfect ending of a career that had spanned 354 wins, with 40 impressive wins and $203,048 in lifetime earnings. To take a horse's harness off for the final time and give him one last look at the racetrack they have loved for so many years, is indeed a privilege like no other.

This special story was published in the March 2024 of Hoof Beats *magazine, the nation's largest harness racing publication. One would think that going out with a win would have been a perfect ending to the story of the octogenarian and his noble steed, but not for Mr. Nadeau and Putty. Slipping back into his green and white silks and dusting off Putty's harness, the pair competed in 7 more races of the Maine Amateur Driving Club series. (There is no age cap on horses in amateur races in harness racing.) The grey took his last look at the racetrack, but Nadeau looked for another horse to drive! He briefly owned a classy gelding, N Expense, who took him to the winner's circle twice in their seven starts together, and ended the 2024 race meet with the 4-year-old mare, Arariya. Another seven starts with her resulted in a single win, ironically at Farmington Fairgrounds (Maine) where he first slipped his hands into those soft leather hand holds with his first horse, Billfold, and caught the racehorse fever, 58-years ago. As he crossed the finish line that warm September day, the announcer pointed out to the fans, watching the green and white silks soar across the finish line, "Ladies and gentlemen, the age difference of the pair you see before you coming into the winner's circle is an astonishing 99 years between horse and driver." The fans cheered and the spritely old gentlemen headed back to the barn. Robert Nadeau replied, "I don't know why everyone is making such a big deal, I'm only 86!"*

Mr. Robert Nadeau celebrated his 87th birthday on December 26, 2024.

As told by Robert Nadeau,
Saco, Maine.

A DAY IN MY LIFE

Picture it: You're at the racetrack. You have a racing program in one hand and a winning ticket (you hope) in the other. The horses thunder past you, mere feet from your place along the rail near the finish line. Manes and tails flowing, hooves pounding, hearts racing, and those famous words echo throughout the grandstand, "AND THEY'RE OFF!" Before you know it, the horse you picked crossed the finish line, a winner! The thrill, the excitement, the rush! And just like that, the race is over. Do you ever wonder what happens back in the barn? One Standardbred trainer/driver tells his story.

A glimmer of light peeking through my window is telling me it's time to grab my morning coffee and head to my truck. As a trainer of Standardbred racehorses, I believe an earlier start is a good thing; the days are long enough. My passion for training and racing horses began at an early age. I was 15-years old in 1975, working at my cousin's stable. After three months of cleaning stalls, my dream of being a driver finally came true. Sitting behind these amazing animals was a feeling like no other—I was hooked! I had been bitten by the "horse bug," as they say. I passed my driver's test after some tedious studying and began racing horses at 16 years old.

I arrive at the barn, the horses recognize the rumble of my tires and the hum of the engine and, before I can even walk in, I'm greeted by nickers of "Good morning" and eager tossing of heads patiently waiting for breakfast. The horses fed, the barn is quiet once again, except for the sounds of grain crunching and an occasional feed tub bouncing off the wall. I enjoy the solitude, cleaning stalls and one-by-one, looking over my horses, observing each of their habits—some of them not necessarily good, the occasional horse would flip its grain out and eat off the floor!

71

I bring out my first horse of the day. He enjoys the brush, especially on his neck, and a big stretch from him tells me he's ready for the task at hand. The soft black harness is carefully fitted and he willingly accepts the bit, looking forward to his daily exercise on the racetrack. The air is crisp this morning. Cool morning air gives my horses a little extra spring in their step; a swish of the tail and a few swift kicks of the hind feet is telling me that my horse is feeling good this morning. After about 5 jog miles around the track—some days we go strength conditioning miles—it's time for a nice warm bath and a little walk on the lead rope for some fresh, green grass. I'm always observing my horses and this is another opportunity to make sure they are in good health after their exercise.

After about ten minutes of grazing, it's on to the next horse. The horses are put away and happily munching on a flake of hay and a can of grain, but I have to clean my equipment with a mild soap and a good sponge before I get to head home for some lunch, and maybe a 30-minute nap.

No day is complete without some bookwork. Each horse has its own diary, containing notes on how they were doing, tidbits on their training miles, upcoming races, details on shoeing, dates when they were wormed, vaccinated, or saw a vet.

Most of my younger horses would make their first starts at the county fairs of Wisconsin, where the friends you saw every summer were like family. The first races of the season were spent catching up on stories with the people you've known for years. After some education, some of my horses were showing enough talent to head to the big-time track in Chicago. Those are long days, getting up early to do chores at the barn before shipping in to race, unloading horses and equipment at the track, racing, cooling out, and getting home in the wee hours of the morning, just in time to start morning chores all over again.

Whether it was racing at a small county fair or under the bright lights in Chicago, I always felt a sense of pride watching one of my horses develop from a young, inexperienced animal to a proud, developed racehorse on their first trip to the winner's circle.

It's later in the afternoon, bookwork is finished and it's time to head back to the barn for evening chores. One by one, they are taken back out for another stroll and some fresh, green grass. Most of their day is spent in the stall and they appreciate the sunshine therapy. Suppertime consists of a can of good quality grain, fresh hay, and a bucket of cool, clean water. A calm comes over me as I take one last walk through my barn for the night, the barn is swept, the horses are clean, and the equipment hangs, shining and smooth, waiting for a new day. My truck tires rumble and my engine hums as I head home for the night.

It's the next morning and a glimmer of light peeking through my window is telling me it's time to grab my coffee and head to my truck to do this job of training horses that I love!

*Written by Edward A. Cockroft,
Richland Center, Wisconsin.*

Ed Cockroft drove his first horse at the Iowa County Fair in Mineral Point, Wisconsin, at the age of 16, against some of the state's finest drivers. He has dabbled in the harness racing business for nearly four decades, driving horses throughout the Midwest at dozens of racetracks. His training expertise resulted in a win and a second in the prestigious Incredible Finale Series at Maywood Park in Illinois. He had a knack for developing young horses, and many of the horses he trained went on to accomplish great things. His legacy will always be remembered at his home track of Richland Center, Wisconsin, where he piloted four winners in a row on one race card. Known all over the Badger State as "Fast Eddie," he racked up an impressive 53 wins, 47 seconds, and 61 thirds in 342 starts. He even drove a few winners for the author, and the pair have been in each other's lives for nearly 20 years.

HORSES IN HEAVEN

God was looking for a racehorse, to fill His heavenly barn.

Just when He thought He'd been everywhere,

He found that Gotham farm.

"I need a horse," He said, that raced with all his heart,

one that gave it all he had, his best with every start.

Every trip around the track, he kept his driver safe.

They loved the thrill, the sport, the speed,

no matter where they placed.

The county fairs a memory, his once swift legs at rest,

God took him home to prove to us, He only takes the best.

An empty stall and memories, the years went by too fast.

He's joined the greats and champions of harness racing's past.

So hang his halter on its peg and put away his tack.

He's in the Almighty's hands, racing on God's racetrack.

In loving memory of Space Commander 1991-2024

Written by Amber Sawyer

*Standardbred Space Commander and Van Nelson of Gotham,
Wisconsin, shared 31 years together before his passing in the
summer of 2024. He raced primarily on the Wisconsin, Illinois, and
Michigan county fair circuit for the majority of his 137 starts. With*

Mr. Nelson as his regular driver, the pair racked up an impressive five consecutive Wisconsin Pacer of the Year Awards, one of the state's highest honors. The bay gelding made his last start on September 2, 2001 at the Walworth County Fairgrounds in Elkhorn, Wisconsin.

After his retirement was announced, his harness was removed in front of a crowded grandstand and he left his last hoof prints on that clay racetrack. He boasted an impressive 43 wins, 25 seconds, and 21 thirds with lifetime earnings of $13,409 and a lifetime mark of 2:01 at the age of 6. At 33 years old, he passed away peacefully at that Gotham farm where he had lived nearly all his life.
Mr. Nelson thought back fondly to his many trips around the racetrack with the horse he purchased so many years ago.
"He may not always have been the fastest, but no matter where we were in the race, I always knew he would take care of me. There aren't too many horses like him."

THE CHESTNUT

The misfits. The hopeless. The outcasts. The last chances. The troublemakers. Aryanna Kuchta has a reputation for taking in the horses that people have given up on. She's never been afraid of a challenge. There's never been a horse she's turned away. "My barn doors are always open," she always says.

Surprisingly, Aryanna never grew up with horses. She spent her childhood reading every horse book and watching every horse movie she could find, bound and determined to be just like all those lucky people who filled her imagination with visions of riding bareback with the wind flying through her hair and her arms wide open. She longed to hear the nicker of horses nibbling grass in the early morning hours or the rhythm of hoof beats galloping up to a white fence to greet her with eager muzzles, searching for a crisp apple.

"Someday," she told herself.

She started working at the local stable to fulfill her horse fix, in exchange for riding lessons. At 10 years old, she finally got her first horse. Since then, she's touched the lives of so many horses, but one fiery redhead came into her life that she'll never forget.

"People who have given up on their horses often call me up ," Aryanna explained. "They aren't always bad horses. They are just misunderstood."

She got a random phone call. A chestnut gelding, too much for his owners, was available. Would she take him? He had nowhere else to go. She didn't like the alternative if he didn't come to her farm. Time went by with no word after that initial phone call. She assumed they had changed their minds and put the chestnut gelding in the back of her mind. One day, out of the blue, a truck and trailer made its way down her driveway and out stepped a towering, nearly 17-hand, red gelding—as red as the sky at sunset, with three white socks and a bright white blaze down his face. The sheer size of him was intimidating. The shipper handed Aryanna a lead rope, waved goodbye, and left. And just like that, with no warning, the thick, copper gelding was hers and the pair stood in the driveway together, watching the rig make its way down the driveway, leaving just as quickly as it had arrived.

Now, it was time for the real work to begin.

The best place to start is always at the beginning. After a few days to settle in and some light ground work, Aryanna wondered, *where was the problem?* She crawled on his back with nothing but a rope halter, and up in the air he went on his powerful hind legs. The massive, fiery horse came back down, expecting a response from his rider, but Aryanna was still and determined not to be intimidated.

The big red horse, who had been named Finn, came down looking confused. As their lessons continued, every time Finn would act up, the brave Aryanna was able to coax him back down, never letting him get the best of her. "As long as your attention was on him, he would be fine. I think it was his sheer size that stopped everyone from trying to figure him out," she said.

It was just a fortunate accident the day she found out just how special her new, big, red horse really was. They were out on a ride one day, Aryanna was testing Finn's limits, wanting to see just how much he could really do now that they were becoming more comfortable with each other. Finn was able to perform a perfect sliding stop, most popular in horses that have competed in reining, proving to his rider that he was so much more than the bouncy red horse she had started with just a few months before. Finn had obviously been a show horse at one point in his life, as he perfected his working trot, his canter, spinning, and lead changes. His second career with Ariana had begun. He was winning ribbons in everything he was put in, but he excelled the most at Liberty riding. The freedom of not having a saddle and a simple rope around his neck definitely agreed with him. He had found his calling.

Aryanna and her auburn companion began their Liberty career, dominating the competition. With his jitters behind him, Finn even became her main lesson horse at her farm, and, one by one, they were educating children by the dozens about Liberty riding; their motto being, "Just because someone had a rough start does not mean a rough ending."

Now the perfect horse for building a person's self-esteem, the big, red gelding does his best to take care of even the least experienced rider. His remarkable transformation has proven to the world that we need to look for the good because it will always prevail over the bad.

As told by Aryanna Kuchta,
Woodstown, New Jersey.

THE TRIO

"Omne Trium Perfectum"
–Latin Phrase meaning everything that is three is perfect.

The number three is everywhere in life. Three times the charm. Life, liberty, and the pursuit of happiness. Rock, paper, scissors. Goldilocks and the Three Bears, the Three Little Pigs, and the Three Stooges. The genie always grants three wishes. Some of life's most powerful phrases have just three little words. *I love you. I forgive you. Live, Laugh, Love,* and the infamous *Seize the Day*. Heather Rowley also believes in the power of three.

It all started when she joined 4H at the age of eight and, with the help of her parents, purchased a little Shetland weanling and named him Stormy, after her favorite story, "Misty of Chincoteague." The price she paid was a whopping $25. She showed him in saddle seat and halter showmanship, where he placed 2nd as only a yearling. She knew he was going to be something special, even with his feisty attitude. Stormy was awarded the Grand Champion as a 3 year-old with 12 year-old Heather, beating out all of her high school-aged competitors. They were an unstoppable pair.

Her favorite judge, Mr. Tom Long, helped shape her showing career. Constructive criticism was his forte. "Showing horses is a dance. Let the judge lead." It was a saying that Heather lived by, especially when little Stormy won Reserve Champion at only 6 years-old.

Their celebration, unfortunately, was short-lived, and within the hour, triumph escalated to a horrific tragedy. While she was waiting for her next class to begin, Heather stopped with Stormy at the outside of the arena to watch her friend, who was showing her pony and cart, when the horse spooked and the driver was thrown from the cart. Horse and cart uncontrollably came crashing through the fence towards Heather and Stormy. She stood frozen in her tracks, but courageous little Stormy reacted and stepped in front of her, the shaft of the cart buried in his chest. She was rushed to first aid, where soon after, she got the news. He was gone almost instantly, sacrificing himself to save her, who would surely have been struck.

"Stormy saved my life," Heather was grateful but disheartened. "I'll always be in debt to him. There will never be another Stormy."

Three months later, after the catastrophe, Heather and her family were on the search for another horse. Knowing all too well, there was no replacement for her heroic Stormy, she turned to Bruce Becker of Northern Illinois for a new horse. Mr. Becker brought out a beautiful stallion named Georgetown's Tomcat. Heather's 14-year-old heart fell in love. "Being that he was a stallion, my parents said no, but my stubborn teenage mind promised myself I would own him someday."

The next best thing was Rocket's Rockin Robin, a gelding Shetland. Rocket, age 8, had come directly from a show barn where he had one job. "He was pretty high strung," Heather recalled. "The only time he ever got out was to go to the show ring, and then he had to be all business."

Rocket had never learned how to be a pet. He was even afraid of carrots! She made the nervous boy into something special; Grand Champion for 4 years running before she aged out of 4-H. They were still proving themselves in open shows until he passed at age 23.

After Rocket, the flame for horses fell silent in Heather. She didn't know if she had it in her to add fuel to that fire after Stormy and Rocket. Nearly two decades later, a spark was ignited. Her friend Brande found a palomino stallion, and ironically, as the third show pony Heather would own in her life, had been named Trilogy. It was fate. The flame in Heather was burning as bright as ever as she was back in the show ring, this time with Trilogy, boasting four Reserve Championships and one Grand Championship. Brande even found Heather a second horse, a filly named Green Creek's Supreme Ikon. Heather looked at her papers—a granddaughter to her teenage crush, the stallion she had fallen in love with so many years ago, Georgetown's Tomcat! It was a heartwarming chapter to her tragic beginning in her love of horses so many years ago. She and Trilogy were now an unstoppable team, with no end in sight. "Trilogy is my Palomino Stormy. It's like he's come back to me in a different color." She exclaimed.

The horses of your past are always a part of you. You carry them with you, and sometimes, when you dream, you can feel their cadence.

As told by Heather Rowley,
Janesville, Wisconsin.

THE ULTIMATE PRIZE

We all have that once-in-a-lifetime horse that has a special place in our hearts. The one that unites us, excites us, and leaves us in utter amazement. Harness racing pacer, Prize Art, had only earned $950 lifetime when trainer Ronnie Roberts handed over $1250 for the small, black gelding. He and partner, longtime friend, Reed Remley, a well-respected farrier from Wisconsin, decided to take a chance on the 2 year-old, and hopefully have a little fun racing at the betting tracks in Illinois. Both horsemen had known each other for nearly 30 years. The fiery little black was discovered when he was seen flying, almost uncontrollably, around the racetrack at Hawthorne Racecourse in Illinois with another trainer.

Ronnie was always looking for a challenge, and Prize Art looked to be the perfect project and, at just the right price. He had only raced a few times, averaging only $200 per start in his five lifetime races. There was only one direction to go: up, and the work began. Prize Art needed to put on some weight and get healthy if he was ever going to prove himself as a racehorse. Reed's wife and Prize Art's co-owner with Ronnie's wife, Alice, Mindy Remley, remembered the feisty little gelding best. "He was cute on the outside, but his attitude was a whole other story."

Now that he was healthy, his love for racing quickly shown through. "He was all business on the racetrack with a big attitude to match," she said. He was improving with every start, and just three short months after his purchase, Prize Art won his first race, and the rest was history. He was taken out of claiming races for fear of losing him. The quartet of owners, excited at their improving prospect, paid him into some high money Stakes races.

"He was the one you dream of," Mindy said. "A horse doesn't know how much you paid for them. They will give you their all."

Prize Art and his four-some were even featured in *Horseman And Fair World* magazine for their rags-to-riches story. The entire country was in awe of the little pacer that could. With a win in the Cubs Pacing Series with a purse of $10,000. He had another less than two weeks later in the Booze Crusin' Pacing Series Elimination for a purse of $12,000, and a third win in the final for a purse of $53,500. Prize Art was quickly adding to his bankroll and was being driven by some of the nation's finest and most talented drivers.

As they say, "All good things must come to an end," and the Robert/Reed combo was given an offer for their mighty little gelding that they couldn't refuse: $150,000, an obscene amount for a small-time farrier, his wife, and their trainer. It was the bittersweet ending of a journey that none of them would ever forget. Prize Art had taken them on the ride of a lifetime.

In loving memory of Reed Remley 1957-2018

As told by Mindy Remley,
Evansville, Wisconsin.

WINNING OUR RACE

"When we listen to our horses, they tell us a lot."

- Breanna Jerde.

Pepto's Treasure, aka Percy, was just beginning his barrel racing career when the 6 year old Quarter Horse/ Paint gelding flipped in the trailer. Hearing that your horse has a fractured pelvis would most likely have an owner looking for a new rodeo horse, assuming their career was over, but not Breanna Jerde. "I knew Percy was a one person horse, and I was his person," she said.

With six months of stall rest in his future, a relaxing vacation for some horses, but not for Percy, whose personality was too big for his stall.

"After the first month, he finally relaxed a little and finally realized he had to be in there for his own good," she said. "I started visiting him three times a day. Our bond grew close; closer than most people were with their horses." If the two of them could make it through this, they could make it through anything. This was the ultimate test. After seven months of stall rest, it was time to start the rehabilitation process. Five minutes of handwalking daily, then ten, upgraded to some light lunging, and finally, Breanna and Percy were up to some light riding. Just after a year into the injury, they were back to the barrels, and Percy's time was just a second off the fastest time, in a 3-D finish. He loved his job so much and gave everything he had to it. It wasn't long before he sored up again. "I knew him like the back of my hand, and I knew something just wasn't right with him." Breanna tried everything. She went to five different vets in Wisconsin; she tried laser therapy, shockwave therapy, and acupuncture. An X-ray revealed that the gelding's fracture had healed crooked, putting too much pressure on his hip when he went to turn that first barrel. "I knew he was a natural, and he loved it. We always tried to get his bad side out of the way first. Everyone knew if he made it out of that first turn, Percy would be a force to be reckoned with the rest of our run." Percy wasn't ready to give up, and neither was Breanna. She kept searching for answers. After her graduation from Equine Massage School and many ups and downs three years after his injury, Breanna finally found her and Percy's saving grace in the Electro Equiscope, something completely new to the Wisconsin equine world. "It uses electrical micro current throughout the body to find and target damaged cells," Breanna explained. She was willing to do anything she could to help Percy be able to what he loved, finding the best vets she could, traveling as far as Texas to see some of the most skilled vets in the country. It was there that she learned Percy also suffered from "kissing spine," where the vertebrae rub together. "I knew the best thing I could do for Percy was to get myself certified as an Electro Equiscope Technician, so I could learn how to use it properly. We had to get back to the Rodeo!"

Twelve sessions in four weeks with her new machine and the pair was, once again, off to the races; the barrel races that is! A top ten finish (out of 100) proved that Percy was back and better than ever. But, would it last? Another rodeo in Manawa (Wisconsin) over the 4th of July the duo placed 13th, just a tick off the money. Percy just kept getting better. Full of confidence, it was time to tackle one off of Breanna's bucket list, a win at a Pro Rodeo. She had her gelding as sound as he'd ever been, and his success was advancing her Electro Equiscope business; it was time to put another feather in her hat. It was a dark and rainy night in their hometown of Wausau (Wisconsin) at the Wisconsin Valley Fair. The arena was nothing but an ocean of mud. All her friends and family were in the stands, braving the downpour to watch. Breanna tipped her cowboy hat down to keep off the rain, tightened her grip on the reins, adjusted herself in the saddle, and turned Percy loose. He blazed by the first barrel perfectly, nailing the turn, shot to the 2nd, then the 3rd and sailed for the wire, a full three-tenths of a second faster than any other horse that night. The entire crowd, soaked from head to toe, was on their feet cheering as Breanna and Percy took their victory lap.

As told by Breanna Jerde,
Mosinee, Wisconsin.

MOLLY

God once said, "I need someone strong enough to pull a cart, but gentle enough to love a child, willing enough to work beside his master in the fields, but caring enough to raise a newborn foal, smart enough to protect his owner, and passionate enough to love his family, loyal enough to devote his life to serving others, but deserving enough of a warm home and to be loved and cared for all of his days." So God created a horse.

The draft foal, a filly, was born on a small farm just outside of Cambria, Wisconsin. A gentleman in dark trousers and a straw hat walked into the barn that morning past the black buggies and carefully polished leather harnesses, lantern in hand, eager for a glimpse at the strong, healthy filly.

She quickly grew into a useful, willing mare and when the gentleman's new son in law, Orla Petersheim, married his daughter, Alice, she was given to the new groom as part of a team to work on his farm just a few miles down the road. Molly, the big sturdy mare, proved to be a useful companion for Orla. She was ready and willing for any job he needed her for and she did it well. She was used for plowing the field, farm work, making hay, and raising foals; as faithful as any horse could be.

Orla, who was also a talented blacksmith, often had several English stopping by throughout the day to tend to their horses' feet and shoeing needs. Jody Calhoun and her husband, Brian, were regular customers of Orla's. They would often make their way up the long gravel driveway, past the neatly kept two story white house and bountiful garden, up to the large, red barn with their team of draft horses, sisters Queen and Jessica, in the trailer for their monthly hoof trimming.

With every visit, there was Molly, happily sunning herself in the field, ears pricked forward, relaxing and watching the visitors to the quaint Cambria farm. It was a tragic day when Jody and Brian lost their beloved Jessica to colic. Queen, her sister, was heartbroken, losing her lifelong partner. They turned to Orla, looking for another horse. Molly, who had served him well, but was no longer able to be bred and was getting too old for field work, deserved a loving home. She went to live with Brian and Jody.

Life was back to normal, but it was short lived. Brian lost his battle to the cancer he had been fighting. Jody's world was turned upside down. She felt paralyzed; devastated. Two draft horses were far too much for her to handle and Orla offered to take both mares. Jody spent her days barely getting out of bed, just struggling to get through the day. She knew she couldn't go on like this and went back to get Molly. "I brought her back home, put her in her stall, held her, and cried. And you know what? She just let me."

Molly knew she was needed, only this time, for a different job. She became Jody's reason to get out of bed every morning. "Molly was meant to be here." Jody was thankful for her gentle giant, "If I needed to just sit in her stall quietly, or to cry, or just to have a listening ear, she was always there for me."

It's amazing how something so overpowering and strong can be so gentle. Molly and Jody live in Montello, Wisconsin, and just participated in their first parade; donning a shiny leather harness and a polished wooden cart. The mare that spent her life working in the fields, raising her foals, and mending a broken heart after a tragic loss, has found her forever home.

Horses are angels sent from heaven to heal broken hearts.

As told by Orla Petersheim,
Dalton, Wisconsin,
and Jodi Calhoun,
Montello, Wisconsin.

In loving memory of Brian Calhoun July 2, 1958-November 2, 2023

THE TALE OF DEREK

There was once a horse named Derek.

Who loved to eat a tasty carrot.

He would eat them here and there,

he would eat them anywhere!

He raced in New Zealand and the United States,

Derek raced all over the place.

He raced here, and he raced there,

old Derek raced almost everywhere!

After a race one day, he was sore.

Derek feared that he could race no more.

One day he met a boy named Paul,

who loved to pet him in his stall.

Derek needed lots of time to rest,

so he could race his very best.

One day in Ironwood, you see,

Derek was driven by Mr. Magee.

His win that day was his very last,

his racing days were in the past.

Derek needed a job and something to do,

now that his racing days were through.

So he wrote a book called "Love to Race "

and it's been read all over the place.

From Madison to Timbuktu,

maybe someday it will be read by you!

Written by Amber Sawyer.

There were lots of times when visiting schools with my first book, Love to Race, I'm asked to also speak to the 4K and kindergarten students.

With my children's book being nearly 40 pages and a little too advanced for that age group, I wrote this poem as a shortened version of the book. I first read it at a school for Read Across America Week, a week-long celebration nationwide in honor of Dr. Suess' birthday.

www.ingramcontent.com/pod-product-compliance
Lightning Source LLC
Chambersburg PA
CBHW051223120626
46547CB00013B/1476